The One-Minute Presentation

Explain Your Network Marketing Business *Like A Pro*

KEITH & TOM "BIG AL" SCHREITER

The One-Minute Presenation
© 2017 by Keith & Tom "Big Al" Schreiter

All rights reserved, which includes the right to reproduce this book or portions thereof in any form whatsoever.

Published by Fortune Network Publishing

PO Box 890084

Houston, TX 77289 USA

Telephone: +1 (281) 280-9800

ISBN-10: 1-892366-86-X

ISBN-13: 978-1-892366-86-3

Contents

PREFACE

Why is it that commercials can present their products clearly in 15 seconds or 30 seconds, and we buy?

Why then do we require a 15-minute or 30-minute presentation to sell our network marketing products and opportunity?

The answer is that commercials use specific "commercial talk" language. By using proven word phrases, they can communicate their message in seconds. We don't know commercial talk. We don't even know that commercial talk exists.

What do we use? Social talk. Why? Because that is what they taught us in school. They thought we were going to have … jobs!

Here is the bad news. Commercials are our competition, and they crush the silly chit-chat social talk we use as networkers.

But the good news is that we can learn commercial talk so we can compete with commercials in the real world.

Anyone can be positive and smile all day long. Prospects will think we are nice. But, if we continue using social talk, prospects won't join our business.

If we want to excel in network marketing, we must learn proven word phrases. Commercial talk works. If we are in business, then we need to start learning commercial talk now.

BIG AL WORKSHOPS

I travel the world 240+ days each year.
Let me know if you want me to stop in your
area and conduct a live Big Al training.

→ **BigAlSeminars.com** ←

FREE Big Al Training Audios

Magic Words for Prospecting

plus Free eBook and the Big Al Report!

→ **BigAlBooks.com/free** ←

WHICH WORDS WILL WE CHOOSE WHEN WE GIVE PRESENTATIONS?

Having a great attitude, being positive, creating a vision board, setting goals, and being super-motivated is nice. But at some point, we will have to **say something!**

Knowing what to say to create rapport, to break the ice, and even to close is a skill. But what are we going to say when we give our presentation to our prospects?

Are we going to read research reports, show PowerPoint presentations, give statistics, and put our prospects into a coma? Or, will we tell our prospects exactly what they want to know? Then our prospects can feel good about the decisions they make.

Information is not the determining factor in our prospect's decision. Shocking? Yes. We will talk more about that in this book. But for now, we want to create interesting presentations. We want to serve our prospects, not bore our prospects.

Is giving presentations intimidating for new distributors? Of course. Having their aunt laugh while they explain the compensation plan is humiliating. It will be the subject of humorous stories for a decade of family reunions. Most of us didn't have a background as professional salesmen when we entered network marketing. So in the beginning, almost every step can cause stress and hesitation.

Here is the good news. Presentations are easy to give. If we learn a few new skills, presentations can be pleasant for everyone in attendance.

So let's get started. With a few new discoveries, presentations can be the most powerful part of our skillset in network marketing.

A STORY WITH A VERY BAD ENDING.

The year was 1972. Armed with great mathematics and physics skills, I had decided to take on a brand-new profession: network marketing.

Because I had studied engineering, I worshipped **information**. I loved information. I collected information. I studied information. I categorized information. I was a nerd.

Of course you had to be a nerd to study engineering. You had to give up your entire social life and interaction with other human beings. Why? So that you had time to memorize even more … information!

At my workshops I often ask the attendees, "Have you ever met an engineer?" Everyone raises their hands. I explain, "We are boring people, personality-free, charisma-bypassed, socially-challenged, and should not be let out in public."

Of course this is a mild exaggeration, but everyone laughs. They realize that engineers need to learn basic social skills first so they can survive in network marketing.

But what is great about engineers is that we immediately understand network marketing. We understand geometric progression. We have spreadsheets inside our heads. We grasp the potential of the compensation plan immediately.

Unfortunately, we can't execute and make network marketing work. Why? Because we don't have the natural people skills necessary to communicate with others.

We see the potential, but we just can't manage it.

"Have you ever seen an engineer give a network marketing presentation?"

It is hilarious. We talk and talk and talk about facts, proof, and case studies. The prospects' eyes glaze over and roll to the back of their heads. If you are reading this book, you might recall an opportunity meeting when they allowed an engineer to speak.

So in the beginning of my career, here was how my presentation strategy progressed.

Early stages: I read the flipchart to prospects as if they were reading-impaired. Every point was painfully explained and backed up with outside documentation. Nothing was left out. I explained everything about the business in logical order, leading up to the moment where I would ask them to make a decision. It was 45 minutes of monologue, one-way communication that was not to be interrupted.

That didn't work. No one joined.

Everyone said "no" to my perfect presentation. I couldn't figure out the problem.

It never occurred to me that "I" was the common denominator. I was at the scene of the crime at every presentation.

Later stages: I analyzed my dismal results. My conclusion? The only reason that prospects could possibly refuse my awesome presentation was … they needed even more information. With more information, they would feel more comfortable with making a decision.

So yes, you guessed it. Here is what I did.

I increased my presentation to a full 90 minutes of mind-numbing facts, figures and information.

It was an awesome presentation.

And at the end when I asked my prospects for a decision, they would say:

- "Uh, let me think it over."
- "I'm not a salesman."
- "I don't know anybody. I only know three people and two of them hate me."
- "I am too busy."
- "We don't do these sort of things."
- "No time. Too much overtime on my job."
- "I will get back to you."
- "We don't know how to do this."
- "I could never memorize a 90-minute presentation."

There were a lot of ways that prospects told me "no," but I didn't realize they were telling me they **didn't** want to join.

My prospects didn't want anything to do with my business … or me, but they were polite. They didn't want to hurt my feelings. They wanted to tell me "no" in a way that wouldn't make me feel rejected.

The result?

I proved that long, information-filled presentations keep people away from our business. Sitting down with prospects and talking **at them** for 45 or even 90 minutes is a recipe for failure. I can't stand a 30-second commercial. A one-minute commercial prompts me to change the channel.

Yet, somehow I assumed a 45-minute non-stop commercial from an amateur presenter (me) would keep them mesmerized and interested.

What was I thinking???

Obviously, I wasn't thinking much.

We are not dumb.

Here was the basic problem.

In our jobs, we need skills. If we don't have skills, they fire us. Every job requires some skills to get it done.

I had mathematics and engineering skills. Great for my current job. But I decided to join a brand-new profession, network marketing, and I took my logical, information-worshipping engineering skills with me!

It never occurred to me that if I entered a brand-new profession, then I should learn a new set of skills. Weird.

If I had decided to become a doctor, I would have learned a new set of skills of knowing where to cut, or how to administer anesthesia.

If I had decided to become a bomb defusal expert, I would have learned which wire to cut first.

So take a deep breath. No matter what profession we are in before network marketing, we will have to learn a new set of skills. This bit of common sense unfortunately escaped me when I joined.

If we are doctors, farmers, truck drivers, bank managers, housewives, circus performers or even one-eyed bungee-jumping pirates ... we all have to learn a new set of skills if we are going to change professions.

WHAT HAPPENS BEFORE OUR PRESENTATION.

Everybody loves giving presentations. This is the fun part. We get to tell other people about our business. We get to do all the talking.

We love to talk. We love it when people have to listen to us.

That is the easy part.

The hard part is **finding** somebody who will listen to us. :)

Step #1: Getting an appointment.

All over the world, one of the most common questions asked in our business is, "How do I get appointments for my presentations? I need more people to talk to."

Here is why new distributors ask this so often.

Most distributors spend their entire week **looking** for somebody that will listen to them ... instead of spending their entire week giving presentations.

Distributors tell us:

- "I try to talk to my friends, but they don't want to listen."

- "My co-workers run to the other side of the office."
- "I bought some leads. They don't want to talk to me or listen to a presentation."
- "I do all these things, and nobody will give me an appointment."

Sound familiar? Sound like real life?

People are over-marketed to, and are sales-resistant. And to make matters worse, in the beginning of our careers, we say stupid stuff. We don't know what to say, so we just make it up as we go along. It is amazing that anybody shows up for a presentation based upon what we say.

So how do we get appointments with people? If we were to talk to ten people, how many of those ten people would actually give us an appointment for a presentation?

What would you guess? Three appointments out of ten? Two out of ten? One out of ten? Zero?

Getting appointments easily without rejection.

I ask workshop attendees, "How many people here would be happy to get two out of ten people to give you an appointment?"

A lot of people raise their hands. Of course, that would mean eight out of ten people we talked to rejected us. Ugh!

We can do better than that by adding a bit of new skill.

The "principle of reaction" teaches us to ask ourselves questions like this: "What are the words that we are saying that cause eight out of ten people to reject us?"

I have hundreds of pre-scripted invitations that can create a guaranteed "no" response when used. Everyone has some invitations that get similar dismal results. We don't need any extra bad invitations that guarantee failure.

Get 50% success when getting appointments?

But imagine this. What if we learned an invitation that got ... **five out of ten people** to say, "Yes, please give me a presentation!"

How would our business change?

- Would our sponsoring and retailing explode?
- Would we have more fun?
- Would we have less rejection and feel better about ourselves?
- Would it be easier to sponsor new people because we could teach them how to get more appointments?
- Bigger paychecks?
- More people at meetings?
- More belief in your business?
- Better attitude?

Everything would change if we could get five out of ten prospects to say, "Yes, please give me a presentation!"

Unfortunately, we are not going to learn that skill in this book.

I know you are disappointed. Getting five out of ten people to ask for a presentation would be awesome. But instead, we are going to learn a different skill to start this book.

We are going to learn how to:

Get an appointment with almost ten out of every ten people we talk to.

Sound better?

Later, when we are bored, we can go out on our own and learn how to get only five out of ten prospects to give us an appointment for a presentation. :)

But ten out of ten? Almost 100% success?

Yes, it is possible.

Sounds unbelievable.

But we can get an appointment with almost 100% of the people we talk to with just ... 22 words!

And the only reason we are not using these 22 words is that we didn't know them when we started. But we can learn. We learned how to order pizza by telephone. We learned how to use a smartphone. So learning network marketing is not any different. We have to learn a new set of skills.

But first, let's dream. "What would happen if we had the skill to get almost 100% of the people we approach to ask us for a presentation?"

Network marketing would be the most fun profession in the universe!

- We would have unlimited presentations.
- We could afford to be picky. We could refuse to give presentations to people we didn't like.
- There would be no more stress.
- We would spend our entire week **giving** presentations instead of **wasting** our entire week looking for people to give a presentation to.
- Sponsoring new people would be easy because we could give them this skill.

Let's get rid of our skepticism right now.

Here is why we don't get ten out of ten prospects to ask us for a presentation.

Because we **say** and **do** the wrong things. Here is a typical example.

Imagine I am a brand-new distributor. I am standing right next to you at work. We are by the coffee machine and talking for three or four hours.

While we are sipping our coffee, I turn to you, and I say, "Boy, have I got an opportunity for you!" What is the first thing to cross your mind?

"Run. Run. Save myself. Salesman approaching! Hide my wallet! Hide my purse! Think of excuses! Put garlic around my neck!"

Right?

You might become so anxious to get away that you say, "Hey, good time for us to go back to work." Now, that is desperate!

However, this doesn't put me off. No way. I am motivated. I listened to a motivational audio last night. I also chanted affirmations into the mirror before I came to work.

So I continue on. I say,

"Well, it is a great opportunity. Absolutely awesome! You need to come down to this opportunity meeting at the local hotel tonight. Don't worry about the traffic. Don't have dinner with your family. Don't rest after a hard day at work standing by the coffee machine. Instead, come to our incredible opportunity meeting. We are going to give you financial freedom. We will give you time freedom. You can leverage your income into residual income. This will be the changing point in your life. It will be spectacular! Just come to our meeting."

What are you thinking? You are probably thinking, "Man, I really don't want to go down there. Sounds like a cult or some sort of pyramid scheme."

So what are you going to say?

"I am busy."

We've all heard that before, right? Sound familiar? You will answer me by saying, "I am busy tonight. We recently adopted a stray cat and I have to go home and pet it. Plus, I scheduled this evening for changing the air in the tires of my car. I am completely tied up. I can't get away."

But does that bother me or stop me? Oh no. This morning I visualized my goals for 45 minutes while driving to work. Nothing is going to stop me. So I continue,

"Here is your chance to fire your boss, achieve your goals, travel the world. Your family will be proud of you. This is an opportunity to show your love for your family. You can achieve your wildest dreams. You must commit to coming to our incredible, mind-blowing opportunity meeting."

You are thinking, "Yikes! How do I get rid of this jerk? He won't let me alone. I have to think of a reason not to go, or he will continue pestering me all day. Maybe I can find something I don't like about his stupid, time-wasting business opportunity."

So you try by saying, "Well, before I even go down to that opportunity meeting, tell me the name of your company first."

Sound familiar?

I reply, "The name of the company? I really can't do that. Because if I tell you the name of the company, you might prejudge. You might look it up on the Internet and not get both sides of the story. You need to come down to the meeting and see the whole thing at one time. Don't look at a little piece of the pie, but see the whole pie. I don't want you to make a mistake and prejudge. When you come down to the meeting, then I will tell you the name of the company."

Do you think you will come to my opportunity meeting when I won't even tell you the name of the company? Of course not, but I am not discouraged. I sang the company song from the parking lot to my desk this morning. I am super positive.

You still don't want to come so you try this tactic. You say, "Well, tell me a little bit about it first, to see if I am interested, before I waste a whole evening and come down to this meeting."

Sound familiar?

I am ready for this objection, so I quickly answer, "Well, I can't do that. This whole thing is kind of visual. You have to physically be there to see the whole thing at one time so it makes sense. So when you get to our meeting, then you will find out what it is all about. Are you coming?"

And you reply, "No."

Now I am getting desperate. You are the only prospect on my list. I think to myself, "I have to get you to come. I am not getting through to you, so I better go for the heavy guns. I am going for the guilt approach."

I say to you, "Well, I know you don't want to come down, but you owe it to me. We have been friends for 15 years. When you hurt your back last winter, I shoveled your sidewalk. When your daughter needed a kidney, I gave her two kidneys. You owe it to me. Come on down to our meeting."

Now, what are you going do? You think, "Oh gee, I don't want to go to that stupid sales meeting. However, I don't want to give those kidneys back, either."

You desperately need to think of some excuse, so you say, "Well, I'll tell you what. I would like to come to the meeting.

It sounds great, but unfortunately I won't be able to get down there tonight because my car broke down. By the time I take the bus home, I won't have enough time to take another bus to get to your hotel in time."

You know what my reply is going to be. I am going to say, "I will pick you up and give you a ride to our meeting! I will pick you up around 6:30 PM. We will be there by 7:00 PM, get a good seat. Meeting starts at 7:30 PM."

You think, "Ha! 7:30 PM, which means 8:30 PM in network marketing time. Only lasts for one hour, which is 10:30 PM in network marketing time, at which time five people will gang up on me, try to sell me something. I will escape around 11:30 PM at the earliest, be home by midnight, with only five and a half hours of my life wasted."

But to get rid of me you say, "Sounds great. In fact, it sounds so great, so awesome that I'll tell you what I am going to do. Don't even bother to pick me up. I will meet you there. I will catch a ride to the meeting with my neighbor."

And you don't show up at my meeting.

Does this scenario sound a little bit familiar?

Would you agree with me that it is **what we say** and **what we do** that makes a difference?

And that is why we only get one out of ten, or two out of ten, or three out of ten prospects to hear our presentation.

However, we can change all that by learning a simple skill.

Chocolate chip cookies.

If someone gave us a simple, yet awesome recipe for chocolate chip cookies, could we follow that recipe? Of course. It wouldn't matter if we have a good attitude, or if we have or don't have a vision board. All it would take to make these awesome cookies would be the skills to follow the recipe.

It's the same for getting appointments for our network marketing business. All we have to do is follow a simple word-for-word recipe. Anyone can do this. New people. Experienced people. Even skeptical people.

Let's see how we can do this.

How to get appointments almost 100% of the time.

Prospects hate sales presentations. Ever notice that? Why do they hate giving time to salespeople? Let's list a few obvious reasons:

- It wastes valuable television-watching time.

- It might be something they are not interested in.

- They hate change. "Leave me alone. I am fine in my little world."

- They hate salespeople. They talk, and talk and talk.

- They would rather spend the time with their families.

- They don't want to spend money.

- They are busy. They don't want to add more things to their frantic lives.

So when we invite prospects to a sales meeting or presentation, they immediately think, "No!"

Rejection.

If these prospects never hear our sales presentation, our chances of success are slim. Unless we can get an appointment to present our message, we are out of business.

So how do we get an appointment with these sales-resistant prospects?

Easy. And we can get an appointment almost 100% of the time. All we have to do is to go deep into our prospects' minds and see how they think. When we see things from their point of view, appointments are easy.

What prospects are thinking when we try to set an appointment.

- "You are trying to sell me something."
- "I don't want to go to an opportunity meeting. It will be a waste of my time."
- "You are trying to get your high-pressure sponsor to sell me something."
- "I am safe if I don't go on that conference call or webinar. They will convince me to join some scheme."
- "I don't want to spend money on anything."
- "You will embarrass me if I decide not to buy your product or join your business."
- "If I am not interested, you will continue to follow up and harass me until I am disgusted."

Bad thoughts. Really bad thoughts.

Now, we don't want to be manipulative salespeople. We only want an appointment to tell prospects about our business. But we want to avoid rejection.

When we talk to prospects, think about this:

1. Is our prospect leaning forward, looking forward to our presentation?

2. Or is our prospect leaning back, putting up defenses, and trying to avoid a presentation?

In most cases, prospects are leaning back. This is uncomfortable for us and our prospects.

How to get prospects to lean back.

Maybe we try to set the appointment by saying things like:

- "We have an opportunity meeting tonight. It's only a few hours of your time. Want to come?"

- "You need to hear this millionaire on our conference call tonight. Forget about watching your favorite television show. Instead, take an hour to listen to some stranger trying to sell you something."

- "Your job won't make you rich. Let me tell you what you should do with your life. I will get my sponsor on the telephone and together we will tell you what to do."

- "I've got this video you need to watch. And a PowerPoint presentation. Then I will show you how to make money as you watch me draw circles on the whiteboard ..."

See the problem?

Let's get our prospects to lean forward.

Instead of manipulating or trying to sell prospects, let's take a different approach.

We are going to:

1. Relax our prospects.

2. Get our prospects to lean forward, make them anxious to hear our presentation.

Obviously, this looks like a better plan.

Two magic sentences.

We can stop all this drama by using two proven sentences that will make our prospect feel at ease.

Here they are. Only 22 words.

The first sentence goes like this. (Please hold your skepticism until you have read both sentences.)

"I can give you a complete presentation, but it would take an entire minute."

The second sentence is:

"When could you set aside a whole minute?"

Ready to test these two sentences?

I am standing next to you at work by the coffee machine. We have been standing there chatting for three or four hours, drinking coffee and munching donuts. I say,

"Boy, have I got an opportunity for you!" (Okay, not exactly the best opening, but we will work on that at another time.)

You reply, "Oh, no."

I quickly reply, "Relax. Don't worry. Don't panic. It is okay … I can give you a complete presentation, but it would take an entire minute. When could you set aside a whole minute?"

What might you say?

"Okay, how about right now?"

Why does this work?

Now why would you ask me to give you a presentation right now?

First, you are thinking, "Get it over with. Tell me now so I don't have to go to an opportunity meeting."

Second, you might be curious about it. You think, "It is probably ridiculous, but just in case, I better find out what it is. I am a little bit curious. And I can find out the complete story in one minute and have it over with. So what do I have to lose?"

Third, you are thinking, "It's only one minute. I can keep my sales resistance up for a whole minute. I will be safe."

Fourth, you think, "Please give me the presentation now, because I don't want you calling me back later at the house asking for an appointment. Do it now. Get it over with! It would take longer to shake your hand and say good-bye, so tell me now."

Fifth, you realize, "Hey, it is only one minute, so there will be no time for salesmanship, hype, or any of that other junk. Just barely enough time for a few facts. I can say yes, no, or ask a question or two, and this entire drama will be over."

Sixth, you think, "It will take me more than one minute to talk him out of giving me a presentation. Getting the presentation will be the shorter of the two pains."

Seventh, you think, "One minute is much better than wasting an entire evening at an opportunity meeting." (Or on a long conference call or webinar.)

When we say these 22 words, all the pressure and tension is gone. No more drama in our prospects' minds. They relax and hear our story.

Pretty cool, eh? By simply saying:

1. "I can give you a complete presentation, but it would take an entire minute."

2. "When could you set aside a whole minute?"

Almost every prospect we visit will say: "How about right now?"

Still skeptical?

Consider this. I walk up to your door. I am wearing a little salesman hat. It says "Salesman" right across the top. I knock on your door, and I say this. "I can give you a sales presentation. Now, I can give you a long presentation, or I can give you a short presentation. Which one would you prefer?"

Which would you choose? The short presentation, of course.

What if I call you on the telephone? I say, "I've got a great business to tell you about." How would you feel? A bit skeptical and reserved. But what if I continued by saying, "I can give you a long presentation, or I can give you a short presentation. Which one would you prefer?"

Which would you prefer? The short presentation, of course.

Pick up the trend? It isn't the 1970s. In 1970, people didn't have cable television, mobile phones, Internet ... they had nothing to do for entertainment! They had time for our lengthy presentations.

But the 1970s are not coming back. Today, people are busy. We need to respect that. So let's get to the point right away with a short presentation. People have things to do besides listening to our sales presentations.

Too easy?

Yes. And that is why we do it. Because ... it is easy, rejection-free, and our prospects love it. Our prospects are looking forward to our one-minute presentation.

Almost one hundred percent of our prospects are going to say, "How about right now?"

All it took was two simple, proven sentences. We might be thinking, "Wait a minute. Do these same two sentences work over the phone?" Let's give it a try.

Imagine a prospect calls us and says, "Hey, I just saw your business card pinned on the wall at my favorite restaurant. Now, I am not a real person. I don't have a telephone. I am calling for somebody else, so don't ask my real name. But, your business card says I can earn a part-time income from home. So what is it? Tell me a little bit about your business first."

Feel the sales resistance right now? Wow. Th
is defensive and scared. So we disable all that ske͟ͅ.
resistance and fear by saying, "I can give you a complete
presentation, but it would take an entire minute. When could
you set aside a whole minute?"

What is this scared prospect going to say? He will say,
"Tell me now. Right now, while I am on the telephone with
you."

Our prospect no longer has to worry about some high-
pressure salesperson coming to his home, or someone
harassing him by telephone to come to some hotel meeting.
We are going to tell this prospect the whole story, right now,
over the telephone, and he will remain safe.

There is a whole different attitude from our prospect
now. Our prospect feels that we are straightforward and to
the point. The last time our prospect called someone about
an opportunity, he spent 45 minutes on the telephone. And,
our prospect still didn't learn the name of the business or
company.

We are different. We are not trying to manipulate or hide
our business. We are going to tell the whole story in one
minute over the telephone. Our prospect already likes us. :)

Just try this a few times. You will be shocked at how much
more forgiving our prospects will be.

Our prospects will react differently?

Yes. This is how we take stress, tension, and rejection
out of our business. We say the right sentences and our
prospects react differently. By saying these two sentences,

we remove the skepticism and salesman alarms from our prospects' minds.

Now our prospects will lean forward, anxious to hear our presentation.

Can I teach this to my new distributor?

You can teach **anyone** these two proven sentences:

1. "I can give you a complete presentation, but it would take an entire minute."

2. "When could you set aside a whole minute?"

We can teach them to our aunt, our brother-in-law, our co-worker, a college student … anyone!

The best part is that our new distributor will feel **comfortable** saying these two sentences. Yes, comfortable.

Think of how much easier it would be to approach prospects and friends if we knew that our entire presentation would only take one minute!

No rejection. Easy to learn. Fun to say.

We won't need a long training program to get our distributors to learn these two easy sentences.

Earlier we might have been skeptical that getting appointments with almost one hundred percent of the prospects we talk to would be so easy. But now, after we have learned these new sentences, it is easy to see how much more successful we will be.

Let's test this for ourselves.

Think about our "before" picture. Maybe it took us one week to get an appointment with a prospect so that we could give them our presentation.

Let's look at the "after" picture. By using these two sentences, if we talk to enough people, we could get ten appointments in one hour!

Imagine standing by the coffee machine at work. We say these 22 words: "I can give you a complete presentation, but it would take an entire minute. When could you set aside a whole minute?"

Yes, it would be easy to get immediate appointments.

What if we called our warm list of prospects? We would say these 22 words: "I can give you a complete presentation, but it would take an entire minute. When could you set aside a whole minute?"

Yes, we would set a lot of appointments. Most of those appointments would ask for our presentation immediately over the telephone.

Even if we interrupted dinner, our calls for appointments could be successful. We call a relative who says, "I am busy now. We are eating dinner. What is this about?" We could answer, "I can give you a complete presentation, but it would take an entire minute. When could you set aside a whole minute?" And what would our relative reply? He might say, "Well, since you already have me on the telephone, and it is only one minute, tell me now. That is better than calling me back later."

Why would we try to get appointments any other way? When almost everyone says "yes" to our invitation for presentations, life is good.

This eliminates those anxious moments when we feel like salespeople.

A prospect calls us on the telephone. The prospect asks, "What is your opportunity all about?"

We can confidently answer, "I can give you a complete presentation, but it would take an entire minute. When could you set aside a whole minute?"

Now our prospect feels relaxed. He feels that we are honest and to the point. He doesn't have to beg us for information. Plus he can find out the basic information over the telephone, before he decides to make an appointment to meet us in person.

We feel good.

We can make our spouse happy.

Want to cause stress? All we have to do is tell our spouse, "Hey, dear! Tonight I am not going to have dinner. I plan to spend five hours talking to prospects on the telephone. Plus, I will do this every day for the next five days!"

Compare that to this scenario:

Our spouse says, "We have to leave for dinner with friends in 20 minutes. Please be ready."

We don't feel stress. During those 20 minutes, we make another three or four appointments for our business ... before leaving for our dinner. There is plenty of time to build our business if we do it right.

Real life.

When we start our business, we feel a bit embarrassed and shy when asked for a presentation. We envision trying to show PowerPoint slides in a busy restaurant, or giving a standing presentation in our aunt's living room as she laughs at us.

No need to panic anymore. Now when someone wants an immediate presentation, we are ready. We will have a one-minute presentation ready any time we want. So let's continue and learn how to give this short presentation.

Warning! Warning! Warning!

If we don't use these two magic sentences, we will be sentenced to a lifetime of tension and rejection. Ugh!

Getting appointments will be frustrating if we don't use proven sentences to get presentations.

Use these two magic sentences:

"I can give you a complete presentation, but it would take an entire minute. When could you set aside a whole minute?"

Problem solved.

So now, we have the appointment and the appointment is ... right now. What do we do next?

CAN WE GIVE AN ENTIRE PRESENTATION IN ONLY ONE MINUTE?

We might be thinking:

"This appointment skill is the greatest skill ever in the history of Western civilization. This will change the world as we know it. This is the most fantastic thing since the invention of sliced bread and beer. I can't believe how awesome it is, and wow, this is so great, it is going to change my business forever. I will spend my whole week giving presentations instead of looking for prospects. But there is one little flaw …

"How am I going to shorten my presentation to one minute?"

Sounds impossible, doesn't it?

But think back. Didn't we also have the belief that it would be impossible to get appointments with almost one hundred percent of the prospects we talk to?

Everything we don't know sounds hard or impossible. But once we learn how, we believe. So let's get started.

This isn't some trick, but the real thing.

First, let me describe what I mean by a one-minute presentation.

- I don't mean a short infomercial or commercial.
- I don't mean a teaser.
- I don't mean something to get an appointment for later.

What I mean by a one-minute presentation is:

◇◇◇◇◇

A complete, entire, beginning-to-end total presentation with all of the facts the prospects need to know to make an intelligent decision on whether to say, "Yes, I would like to join," or, "No, I don't want to join," or maybe, "I have a question or two."

◇◇◇◇◇

This is not some gimmick or trick. This is the presentation the prospect needs to make an intelligent "yes" or "no" decision.

We simply fulfill our responsibility.

We have an obligation to our prospects. Withholding important facts and information is not servicing their needs. However, overloading them with useless and irrelevant information is equally bad.

We don't want a prospect to come back to us later and say, "Gee, if you had told me everything, I would have joined. I wasted two more years on my job because you withheld important information."

So that is our obligation, sharing the important facts with our prospects.

Our obligation stops there. We are **not** responsible for our prospect's **decisions**. We are not responsible for the spouses our prospects chose. We are not responsible for the jobs our prospects chose. And we are not responsible for their decisions.

Our responsibility is to share the important facts with our prospect and that is it.

Feel relieved?

We don't know our prospects' current circumstances or what kind of issues are happening in their lives. We can't control those factors.

So relax. Our responsibility is to politely share the important facts ... and we are done.

The rest is up to the prospect.

No more rejection, no more stress.

But I want to talk longer.

Understood. We all love to listen to ourselves talk, but our prospects don't. However, remember that the one-minute presentation is only ONE way to give a presentation. There are many other ways to create shorter or longer presentations. We will want to have several options available to us so that we can serve our prospects better.

For most cases, a shorter presentation is best. This gives our prospects a chance to bail out quickly, in case what we have to offer is not for them. This saves them time and stress, and will save us time also.

Think about our own lives. Wouldn't we rather have a one-minute presentation so that we could decide if we wanted more information or not?

This book is about the one-minute presentation. So let's start learning how to do that now.

THE BASICS OF THE ONE-MINUTE PRESENTATION.

We think, "I can't give a one-minute presentation. I have too much to explain."

That is exactly the problem. Most of what we say in our presentation … our prospects don't want to hear.

There are only two ways to get our presentation down to one minute.

Option #1: Learn to talk really, really fast.

Option #2: Take some things out of our presentation.

Talking fast is a poor option. There is no way we can get our presentation details into a minute. And even if we did that by talking extremely fast, no one would understand us. So let's take Option #2.

Let's start by taking some things out of our presentation.

Our presentations contain facts, figures, and information.

But if our prospects are not going to join, do they need to know those facts, figures, and information?

No.

And if our prospects do join, they can learn those facts, figures, and information later in training.

Remove company trivia.

If we talk about our company, we can take out the name of the company founder, the company founder's credentials, the people on the board of directors, the profit and loss statement for 2004, the number of new distributors sponsored in May of 2009, the size of the executive conference table, the year when we were the 37th fastest-growing company in the Costa Mesa region, and every article ever written about our wonderful company. And yes, we don't have to show the PowerPoint slide with a picture of our company's office building.

Whew! That is a relief. Because if our prospects are not going to join, they don't need all that data. And if our prospects join, well, we will have plenty of time to show them these details later.

Taking out all these details about the company makes things a lot easier. And, we free up a lot of time too.

Remove products and services trivia.

But what about our products or services? Can we remove a lot of wasted facts and information there also? Sure. Let's take out the name of the rock formation in China where the special herb is grown that is picked by leprechauns at midnight when the dew point is just right. Let's remove the type of ink that is used on our labels, the number of employees who wear lab coats on Thursday afternoons, the 650 testimonials, the 44-page research report from the University of Wisconsin, etc. We can remove the dates of the billing cycles of our services, and the type of manufacturing equipment used to create higher viscosity in our skin creams.

Because if our prospects are not going to join, they don't need all that data. And if our prospects join, we can share this information later.

Now we've freed up even more time. Plus, our presentation is getting a lot simpler.

Remove compensation plan trivia.

What about all the time we spend describing the compensation plan? We can remove the description of the qualifying volume, the bonus volume per product or service, and the number of qualified customers needed to advance to the next rank. We don't have to mention every advancement position in the compensation plan.

Let's ask ourselves, "Did we understand our company's compensation plan the first time we heard it?" Probably not. And do we understand it even now? In many cases, no. So all the percentages and volume requirements are things we learned later, after we made our decision to join our business.

So let's take out the compensation plan details. Removing all this information will work for most prospects. The exceptions are the engineers, accountants, and trivia collectors.

Because if our prospects are not going to join, they don't need to know all the details of the compensation plan. And if our prospects join, well, we can give them this information after they enroll.

By taking out these facts, figures, and information, we can now get our presentation down to one minute.

Wow. That change alone would make a huge difference in our business.

But what information does the prospect really want to know?

Ah, there is the million-dollar question. What information should we keep in our presentation? Our prospects need enough information to make a preliminary decision:

Choice #1: I want to join your business.

Choice #2: I don't want to join your business.

Choice #3: Your business sounds good, but I have a question or two.

Prospects make their preliminary decision quickly. Our prospects want to see the big picture first to decide if our business interests them or not. This big-picture presentation has to be fast and must answer three basic questions.

OUR PROSPECTS' THREE BASIC QUESTIONS.

At this point, our prospects only want the answers to three basic questions. If we answer these three questions, our prospects will have enough information to make that preliminary decision.

Remember, if our prospects make a decision to join your business, those other facts, figures, details, and information can be learned later in training.

These are the same three questions we would ask if **we** were looking at a business opportunity.

Simple, yes?

Here are the three questions we must answer:

Question #1: "What kind of business are you in?"

Question #2: "How much money can I make?"

Question #3: "Exactly what do I have to do to earn this money?"

That's it!

Answer all three questions in only one minute? Still hard to believe we can give prospects enough information to make an intelligent decision?

Well, one minute is a long time if we are efficient.

To relieve our doubts, I will demonstrate a one-minute presentation that answers all three basic questions ... in less than ten seconds!

I will answer all three questions in ten seconds, and then take a 50-second coffee break.

Now if I can do this in ten seconds, don't you think that we can do it in a whole minute? I think so.

Just ten seconds, and they will have all the facts they need to know to make an intelligent decision to say,

1. "Yes, I want to join."

2. "No, I don't want to join."

3. "I have a question or two."

Let me give an example of a one-minute presentation that is outside of our industry. This way we can see the one-minute presentation through the eyes of a prospect.

Here is the example:

◇◇◇◇◇

"We are in the car relocation business. You can earn an extra $100,000 a year, and all you have to do is steal cars. Well, what do you think?"

◇◇◇◇◇

That was quick, wasn't it? Less than ten seconds!

Our prospects received the answers to their three basic questions:

1. "What kind of business are you in?" (We are in the car relocation business.)

2. "How much money can I earn?" (You can earn an extra $100,000 a year.)

3. "Exactly what do I have to do to earn that money?" (All you have to do is steal cars.)

Because our prospects received the answers to these three questions, they can make an immediate decision. They could answer by saying:

- "Yes, my cousin does this already. So how do I join?" (I want to join.)

- "No, it is not for me. My mom won't let me." (I don't want to join.)

- "I have a question. Do I have to steal cars? Or could I steal motorcycles instead?" (I want to join, but I have a quick question.)

Enough information.

We didn't have to:

- Give the history of auto theft.

- Give testimonials from successful car thieves.

- Insist they come to an opportunity meeting and meet high-achieving car thieves.

- Show them PowerPoint slides of some of the biggest moments in vehicle relocation history.

- Tell them how many cars they had to steal to move up in the compensation plan.

In less than ten seconds, our prospects know if they want to join or not.

If our prospects don't want to join, we finish. At the end of the ten seconds they say, "No, it's not for me." Here is what we could say. "Hey, let's go to a movie. Let's go shopping." It is over. They are adults. They made up their minds. We completed our obligation of letting them know about the opportunity. We don't have to pester them forever.

Does that feel refreshing?

Now our friends won't walk on the other side of the street every time they see us. We will still be welcomed at weddings, funerals and family reunions.

If our prospects want to join, we can schedule training for later in the week. For now, we will show them how to enroll. The hard part of sponsoring is over.

And if our prospects have a question or two, let's be polite. Let's answer their questions as honestly and clearly as we can. For example, if our prospects says, "Does your company's name start with a vowel? I hate vowels!"

We would answer, "Yes, our company's name starts with a vowel."

If our answer disqualifies our prospects, that is okay. Now is the time to find out.

That simple?

We might be slapping our foreheads and thinking, "Whoa! You mean we don't have to give a 20-minute, 30-minute, or three-hour presentation? We could give our prospects the whole story in one minute and get on with our lives? That would be excellent."

This one-minute presentation would be wonderful over the telephone. No more misleading invitations. Direct answers for our prospects.

This one-minute presentation would be wonderful over a cup of coffee. No need to extend the conversation further if they are not interested.

This one-minute presentation would be wonderful before the opportunity meeting started, or even before inviting them to the opportunity meeting.

So let's take a look at the first question in our prospects' minds.

Question #1: "What kind of business are you in?"

Isn't that a fair question? In other words, are we in agriculture or real estate? Are we in nutrition? Are we in car racing? Are we in sports medicine, insurance? What kind of business are we in? Our prospects want to know.

If we were looking for a business opportunity, would we join if we didn't know what type of business it was? No. We would always say, "No."

What if we looked into a business opportunity, and we were unsure what kind of business it was? What would we say? "No." A confused mind always says, "No." Prospects are afraid of what they don't understand.

So the number one thing that prospects want to know is what kind of business we are in.

We must be clear what type of business we are in. If not, our prospects will delay their decision. Why? Because we didn't answer this first question clearly. This is one reason our prospects say, "I need to think it over."

So what type of business are we in?

Banking? Sport fishing? Mechanical repair? Circus performing? Soldier of fortune? Landscaping? Nuclear medicine? Shoe repair?

Our prospects want to know.

Many years ago in Sweden, I asked a networker:

"What type of business are you in?"

He replied:

"I am in the global search for entrepreneurial talent, for time freedom and financial freedom, whereby people can enhance their efforts through multiple streams of residual income, thereby improving their lifestyle ..."

Well, we get the idea. No wonder this networker was having a hard time sponsoring. His prospects had no idea what kind of business he offered!

The hardest question new distributors have to answer is, "What do you do?" A hundred things run through their heads. They break out in a cold sweat. Then something like this might come flying out of their mouths:

"I am a distributor with the Wonderful Company, from the Wonderful City, started in the wonderful year of 1991 by Mr. Wonderful who is a wonderful, wonderful family man, and we have wonderful products, wonderful employees, wonderful shipping, wonderful uplines, wonderful blah, blah, blah ..."

Or are we too vague? Maybe we say:

- "I am in the skincare business." (And the prospect thinks we make bandages for cuts, or maybe we do skin grafts. Or maybe we make yellow latex gloves that protect hands from acid cleaners.)

- "I am in the health and wellness business." (And the prospect thinks that we change bedpans at the local nursing home. Or maybe that we work as a dietitian at the local high school.)

- "I am in the financial services industry." (And the prospect thinks that we are a bank teller.)

- "I am in the telecommunications business." (And the prospect thinks that we build satellites. Or maybe we repair telephones.)

- "I am in the legal services industry." (Do we bring donuts to lawyers? Clean lawyers' offices?)

- "I am in the e-commerce business." (What is that? Does e-commerce come before f-commerce?)

When prospects hear vague sales pitches like these, they think, "I wonder if I should fake a heart attack. Maybe then I can get away."

If we don't know how to describe our business, here is an easy way that should help.

"Which means."

When we describe our business, we should use the "which means" phrase to connect our business to one of our products or services, or at least to a problem that we solve. This helps our prospects understand exactly what we do in our business.

Want some examples?

Try this:

- "I am in the skincare business, which means that we have a moisturizer that makes your skin look 20 years younger in only 45 seconds a day."

- "I am in the health and wellness business, which means that we have a delicious juice that people drink. It helps them wake up an hour earlier every morning feeling like a million dollars, and fall asleep at night within seven minutes of their heads hitting the pillow."

- "I am in the financial services industry, which means that we help families lower their mortgage, credit card, and car payments. Now they will have more money for fun things and retirement."

- "I am in the holiday travel business, which means I show families how to take five-star holidays for the price of a good hotel room."

- "I am in the utilities business, which means I help homeowners get a great price on their utilities, so they don't have to shop and compare new deals every month."

- "I am in the cosmetics business, which means I help women get the coordinated look they want that they can't get by buying random cosmetics."

- "I am in the water filter business, which means I show people how to eliminate all those nasty things that come out of the kitchen faucet."

See the difference? Now our prospects know exactly what kind of business we are in.

Don't forget those magic words, "which means." These words will guide us to a better description of the type of business we are in.

Getting it right.

This is important. We need to take the time to make sure we can describe the kind of business we are in clearly. If our prospects have to ask us for clarification, that is our clue to go back and make our description better.

If our description is too long, it will sound like a sales pitch.

If our description sounds exaggerated because we used words like amazing, incredible, ground-breaking, perfect, patented, proprietary ... well, our prospects will have their internal sales alarms blaring.

We want to make our description sound normal. We are not trying to sell our prospects. We are answering our prospects' internal questions.

Take a moment to write out exactly how you would describe your business to your prospects. We will need this later as we assemble our one-minute presentation.

Now, on to question #2.

QUESTION #2: "HOW MUCH MONEY CAN I MAKE?"

I am certain we would ask this question if we were looking at a business opportunity. It is a fair question.

This question is easy. We will pick a figure that we feel matches our prospects' desires. For someone looking to earn a few hundred dollars a month part-time, we will describe one income. For someone who wants to quit his job and build a fortune, we will quote a different income.

We want to match what our prospect is looking for. If we quote thousands of dollars of extra income to someone earning minimum wage, it may seem unbelievable or unrealistic. Conversely, if we quote $100 extra a month to someone looking for a full-time business, that would be discouraging.

So how do we know how much income to describe?

Use our common sense.

If we don't know how much income the prospect is looking for, ask! During our conversation, we could ask this question:

"If you were to have an extra income with our business, how much extra income would you be looking to earn?"

However, most times we will know. For example, imagine our prospect overheard us talking about how our brother is earning an extra $500 a month. The prospect says, "Hey, that sounds interesting. How does that work?" We now know how much money to describe. We will do some examples of this later.

But now, on to that third question.

What is the final question that the prospect needs to have answered to make an intelligent decision?

Question #3: "Exactly what do I have to do to earn this money?"

This is the most important question, and most networkers don't answer this question completely. They conveniently skip over this question. Now their prospects have to go home and figure it out for themselves.

Ouch.

This is another huge reason prospects say, "I have to think it over."

As professionals, let's do our job. Let's answer their question: "What do I have to do to earn that money?"

Our prospects may be thinking, "Do I have to have a product party in my living room? Do I have to be a one-eyed bungee-jumping skydiver? Do I have to have a degree in sports medicine? Do I have to have a Ph.D. in chemistry? Do I have to have a certain athletic ability? What exactly do I have to do to earn that money?"

Wouldn't we ask that too?

Our prospects worry, "Well, if what I have to do is going to embarrass me, or if it is something that I can't do, I don't want to try it."

Yes, we have to answer this.

If we don't answer this question in our presentation, how could we possibly expect prospects to make a decision?

Unfortunately, untrained networkers give lame answers to question #3. They give their prospects vague descriptions such as:

- "It is a sharing and caring business."
- "Just talk to people."
- "Be a product of the product."

Ouch. Ouch. Ouch.

We must describe the activity that prospects have to do to earn that money. Then our prospects can make an immediate decision.

We don't want to describe the compensation plan complete with bonus volume, levels of achievement, etc.

Our prospects simply want to know approximately what type of **activity** they must do to earn the money we quoted.

We don't have to read the policies and procedures, describe the minimum 60-day volume required to earn the Star Trek Commander bonus, explain the legal definitions of each term used, etc. All we have to do is tell our prospects generally what they would have to do to earn the money we quoted.

Want some examples?

If we quoted our prospects an extra $300 a month, we could describe their activity as this:

- "All you have to do is this. Every day, pass out a sample of our super-moisturizing cream and this brochure describing how to use it. Then, at the end of about three months, you should have enough people using the super-moisturizing cream that you would earn an extra $300 a month."

- "All you have to do is this. Between you, and everybody you talk to, and everybody they talk to forever and ever ... find about 25 families who want to drink this juice so that they wake up in the morning feeling great. And then you would earn an extra $300 a month."

- "All you have to do is this. Find four families every month who want to lower their utility bill payments and start having some extra money to spend as they like. And then after 12 months, you would have enough customers to earn an extra $300 a month."

See the difference?

Now our prospects know exactly what they have to do to earn that extra $300 a month.

This is polite. We must provide the information our prospects want.

Sounds good, but how do I close or finish this one-minute presentation?

Now it is time for the close. Feel a bit uncomfortable?

The first reason we feel uncomfortable is that we have avoided closing our prospects in the past.

Instead of closing, we talk, and talk, and talk. We hope our prospects volunteer their final decision. We are afraid to ask what they think because we fear rejection.

We think, "Oh, if I ask them to join or buy right now, they might say no. I will feel rejected, and what if I left something out? What if I didn't put something in that would make a difference for them?"

Well, this problem will go away forever, because all we have to do is answer their three questions, and we are done. We answered everything they needed to know, right? So forget this problem.

Here's the second reason that we don't like to close. We don't want to sound like a sleazy salesman who tries to manipulate people by saying things like:

- "Any three-year-old could see this is a good opportunity. Do you have a problem with that?"
- "Don't you love your family?"
- "Do you want to pay by cash or credit card?"
- "Do you want to join now, or tomorrow?"

This is not fair. Forcing people is impolite. So instead, let's give them a chance to make up their own minds if our business is a fit for them today, or not.

We won't need high-pressure, anti-social closing statements. We are having a great conversation, answering our prospects' three basic questions, so this presentation comes to a natural conclusion. Time for our prospects to give us their decision.

Let's look at the first easy and non-confrontational close we can use.

Easy close #1: "Well, what do you think?"

What a relief! Now our prospects can safely tell us what they think. This sounds like a real conversation. And prospects will tell us what they think. They might say things such as:

- "I don't think so. It is not for me."
- "Sounds great. When can we sit down and move this forward?"
- "Seems okay, but I have one more question."

- "I don't want anything to do with better health. My father died young, my grandfather died young, and I want to die young just like them!"
- "Wow. So is there a meeting or something we can go to?"
- "Yes, I would like to do this. Could you explain this to my spouse also?"
- "Makes sense. Show me how to get started."
- "I need to think this over. Is there a brochure I can look at, or a website I can go to? It takes me a long time to make up my mind about anything."

If our business isn't for a particular prospect, great. We sorted this out in less than a minute. And if our business fits what someone is looking for, great. We sorted that out in less than a minute also.

Do prospects make decisions that quickly?

We might think, "Don't prospects have to know everything first, before making a decision?" Of course not. Here is a way of looking at this concept of a preliminary decision.

A new movie comes to our city. How do we make a decision to go to that movie? Do we have to read the entire script before we can decide to see it? No. After we read or hear a few descriptive sentences about the movie, we know enough to decide if we want to see the movie. For example, let's say this was my mini-description of a new movie:

"There are spiders and snakes chasing and terrorizing small children."

Have we already made a decision about this movie? Yes. Most likely we don't want to see this movie. And we don't need any more information to make that decision.

But we might become bored with always saying, "Well, what do you think?" So let's learn another non-confrontational close for variety.

Easy close #2: "And that is it."

What do our prospects think when we say this phrase?

They think, "Oh. We are done. Those are the facts I need to know. I guess I better decide now if this is what I want."

No pressure. No more awkward silences. And best of all, no rejection.

So instead of talking on and on and on, hoping that our prospects will volunteer a positive decision, we can comfortably wrap up our presentation by saying, "And that is it."

Easy close #3: "And the rest is up to you."

Who makes the final decision? Us? Or our prospects?

Our prospects do. So let's find out what their decision is. They will tell us their decision when we say, "And the rest is up to you."

There is no need for high-pressure closes. We stated the facts in our one-minute presentation, and now the next step is up to our prospects. And these words sound pretty final.

We signaled that we are finished, and now it is time for our prospects to decide.

And there is no rejection either. We stated the facts as if we were describing a movie. Nothing bad happens if our friends don't go to the movie we like. And nothing bad happens here if our business isn't for a particular prospect.

Ordinary conversation.

This is how we normally talk to people. Think about inviting someone to a movie, a date, a birthday party, or a weekend outing.

No need for alternate-choice closes or other anti-social pushy closes. It would sound silly for us to invite a friend to a weekend at the beach and close by saying, "Would Saturday at 9:00 AM or Sunday at 1:00 PM be better?"

Knowing how to close is important. We don't want to feel pushy or desperate when we finish. And if we don't know how to close, we will end up talking and talking and talking, hoping that our prospect will volunteer a decision. That is embarrassing and a waste of time.

But should we be more forceful in our close?

No. If we are too forceful, our prospects will not be open with us. So let's imagine this scenario. We say to our prospect, "Well, what do you think?" Our prospect replies, "I am not sure."

Now is the time for us to listen. When the prospect continues the conversation, he may give us a hint of what is going on in the back of his mind. We can find out what is holding him back from making a decision. As an added bonus, this will also show us how we can improve our one-minute presentation in the future.

Sponsoring is not a one-time close. It is the beginning of a long-term relationship. So, in the long term, life will be easier when we get our prospects to volunteer to join.

Now we know the three basic questions and how to close our conversation. Time to combine these pieces and start making our own one-minute presentations.

Let's put it all together.

Ready for some examples?

We are standing by the coffee machine at work. One of our co-workers says to us, "I hear you started a part-time business. So what is it all about?"

We are ready. We say, "I can give you a complete presentation, but it would take an entire minute. When could you set aside a whole minute?"

Our co-worker replies, "Hey, right now is good." (He feels relieved we won't be trying to get him to a meeting or to some online site with 100 different links.)

Okay, now on to answering those three questions in our co-worker's mind. We say:

◇◇◇◇◇

If you would like to earn an additional $300 per month, you have to do these three things.

Number one: Don't change. Be yourself. Continue to recommend and promote the things you like, such as your favorite movies or music.

Number two: We are in the health foods industry, which means we have this fantastic all-natural juice drink that people drink every morning. It tastes great, builds our immune system, and it makes us feel like we are 16 years old again, but with better judgment. People our age love it.

Number three: All you have to do is let people our age know that we can give up and feel old, or we can drink this juice and feel awesome again. Eventually you will have 30 people drinking the juice every morning, and then you would earn an extra $300 a month.

Well, what do you think?

◇◇◇◇◇

Done.

We answered our prospect's questions. The answers were clear. Now, our prospect can make a preliminary decision if this is for him ... or not.

Notice that there was no real pressure or sales pitch? We just gave the facts, the answers to his questions. And remember, now our prospect can make one of the three choices we spoke about earlier:

Choice #1: I want to join your business.

Choice #2: I don't want to join your business.

Choice #3: Your business sounds good, but I have a question or two.

We didn't ruin any relationships. All we did was answer our prospect's questions in our conversation. The entire process was over in less than one minute. In fact, this particular presentation took about 30 seconds. No one ever complains if we finish our presentation early.

Another example of a one-minute presentation?

Imagine our prospect said, "Yes, I have one minute. Tell me more." We would say:

◇◇◇◇◇

If you want to earn an extra $1000 a month, you have to do these three things.

Number one: Don't change. Be yourself. Continue to recommend things you like such as your favorite music or favorite place to buy clothes.

Number two: Our company is "Diet Pills For Dummies," which means we have a diet pill that people take first thing in the morning, and it makes them shrink all day long.

Number three: All you have to do is loan out this little brochure and sample to two or three overweight people every day. And at the end of about 90 days, you will have enough people using our diet pills to earn an extra $1000 a month.

And, the rest is up to you.

◇◇◇◇◇

Again, clear and to the point. Prospects feel relieved. They won't have that lingering doubt in their minds that comes with unanswered questions.

One more example?

Imagine our prospect said, "Yes, I have one minute. Just get to the point. I don't have much time." We would say:

◇◇◇◇◇

If you want to earn an extra $500 a month, you have to do these three things.

Number one: Don't change. Be yourself. Continue to recommend things you like, such as your personal financial planner or the best place to bank.

Number two: We are Lawyer-on-the-Phone. We show people how to get a lawyer on the telephone to threaten the landlord, get even with the dry cleaners, get a refund from the transmission shop, and fix those stupid speeding tickets they gave you by mistake ... and they do it all for just $25 a month.

Number three: All you have to do is let other people know they won't be blackmailed by high attorney fees by inviting them to our "Save Our Rights" weekly luncheons. So every week, invite a few co-workers or friends to our free weekly luncheons, and most of them will want to be a member just like us. After a few months, you will be earning an extra $500 a month.

And that is it!

◇◇◇◇◇

Done.

Did we answer all three questions? Yes. We told our co-worker what kind of business we were in. We told him how much money he could make. And finally, we told him what he would have to do to earn that money.

Does our co-worker have the information he needs to make a decision? Yes.

Now our co-worker has three choices.

1. Join.

2. Don't join.

3. Ask any questions he might have.

The best thing about this presentation is no matter what choice our co-worker makes, all we have to do is say, "Okay."

If our co-worker wants to join, we say, "Okay."

If our co-worker doesn't want to join, we say, "Okay."

If our co-worker wants to ask some questions, we say, "Okay."

Easy.

Relax. It is not our decision.

Remember, we are not responsible for our co-worker's decisions in his life. We can't worry about the choices he makes. We don't have an agenda. We simply added one more option to our co-worker's life. It is up to him to take advantage of that option, or not.

Can we imagine how many presentations we could give in a day if our presentations took less than a minute?

Can we imagine how much fun giving presentations would be if we relaxed and allowed our prospects to make their own decisions?

Can we imagine how using a one-minute presentation would mean no more rejection because we let our prospects decide their future?

Can we imagine using a one-minute presentation over the telephone? We wouldn't panic if our prospect asked us, "So what is this all about?" We can talk straight to them. We wouldn't have to say, "Oh, you have to invest an evening and come to this meeting to find out the answers to your three questions."

The big benefit.

And what do most prospects think after hearing a one-minute presentation? They think,

- "Hey, I can do this."
- "Well, if you can do this, I certainly can do this."
- "I won't sound like a salesman. I like that."
- "I don't have to memorize a bunch of stuff. This is simple."

Finally ...

Remember that a bad one-minute presentation is preferred by prospects over a perfectly-scripted two-hour presentation. We don't have to be excellent or awesome. Our prospects will appreciate brevity. They can always ask more questions to get more details.

Let's improve.

Once we understand the basics of the one-minute presentation, we can make modifications, improvements, and just have fun. Here are some examples of what we can say after we've made the appointment. So imagine before all of these examples that we have said, "I can give you a complete presentation, but it would take an entire minute. When could you set aside a whole minute?"

◇◇◇◇◇

Water filters.

If you want to earn an extra $1000 a month, you would have to do these three things.

Number one: Don't change. Continue to recommend things that you like, such as your favorite book or your favorite weekend activity.

Number two: We sell water filters. Everyone in the city hates the taste of our water. It tastes like it came out of a washing machine. They don't want to buy cases of bottled water from the store and transport them home every week.

Number three: All you have to do is this. Every day, loan one water filter to somebody who wants better-tasting water.

At the end of the month, 30 people will have tried our water filter. Normally, 10 or 15 of these families will want to keep the water filter.

And then you would earn an extra $1000 a month.

So, what do you think?

Greeting cards.

If you want to earn an extra $400 a month, you would have to do these three things.

Number one: Don't change. Continue to recommend things that you like, such as your favorite television shows or your favorite discount shopping site.

Number two: We sell greeting cards. Everyone hates going to the store to buy overpriced anniversary cards, birthday cards, thank-you cards, and holiday cards. We show them how to order and send their cards from their computer. We print their cards and even put the stamp on for them. Plus, our personalized cards cost less than half of what a generic store-bought card costs!

Number three: All you have to do is this. A few times a week, show people what these great personalized greeting cards look like. Some people "get it" and say, "Wow!" Some don't. For those that "get it," show them how to sign up for our service online.

After a few months, you would earn an extra $400 a month.

So, what do you think?

Debt-reduction services.

If you want to earn an extra $500 a month for traveling, you would have to do these four things.

Number one: Don't change. Continue to recommend things that you like, such as your favorite tax accountant or your dentist.

Number two: We show people how to get out of debt and clear up their credit, without having to pay more money every month. Everyone wants a debt-free life.

Number three: All you have to do is help four families a month enroll on our $25 monthly service plan, so they can start reducing their debt immediately.

Number four: Get your passport updated, because now you will have the extra spending money you need to travel in style.

And then you would earn an extra $500 a month.

And that's it!

◇◇◇◇◇

See the patterns?

First, in all of the one-minute presentations so far, we started with the words, "If you want to earn an extra ..."

Why? These words show us getting to the point. We don't want anxiety accumulating in our prospects. With these words, we answer the question, "So how much money can I make?"

And if we already established how much money our prospects wanted earlier in the conversation, this phrase reminds our prospects of the amount of money we are talking about.

Second, we say, "You would have to do these three things." And yes, we can say "four things" if that explains what we do more effectively.

Wow! Our prospects are thinking, "Great. Right to the point. No wasted time here. And three things, eh? I wonder what those three things are. Please tell me now. This won't be some commercial, long-winded presentation, filled with fluff and useless information. We are getting to the facts now."

And then we start by saying, "Number one."

Our prospects think, "This is going to be simple and clear. Just a quick list of what I have to do. Excellent. I should be able to make up my mind quickly."

Now, can we change the words in these patterns? Of course. But we should at least know why these words are in our presentations. We want to make our prospects feel comfortable by getting to the facts quickly.

This is getting easier, isn't it?

Ready for some more presentations?

◇◇◇◇◇

Healthy coffee.

If you want to earn an extra $500 a month, you would have to do these three things.

Number one: Don't change. Continue to recommend things that you like, such as your favorite donut shop or bistro.

Number two: We are in the healthy coffee business, which means coffee lovers can drink our gourmet coffee every day. They don't have to worry about their stomachs. Plus, our coffee helps them stay fit.

Number three: All you have to do is sit down with three people a day, and talk to them over coffee. At the end of three months, you will have enough people drinking the coffee, or telling others about the coffee, that you will earn an extra $500 a month. Yes, take three coffee breaks every day.

And the rest is up to you!

◇◇◇◇◇

This is starting to sound polite, and more sensible.

Imagine we are talking to a prospect while we wait in line at the bank. The prospect says, "Go ahead, I've got a minute. What is it all about? How does it work? Tell me now." And we say this.

◇◇◇◇◇

Financial services.

Mrs. Prospect, if you want to make an extra $2000 per month, here's what you have to do.

Number one: Don't change. You told me you love helping people, so please continue to make a difference in people's lives.

Number two: We are in the financial industry, which means we help people with their banking, their mortgage, their insurance, and saving for retirement. People aren't experts in these areas, so we can help them a lot.

Number three: All you have to do is concentrate on helping one family a week. Take an evening or two to re-arrange their finances, so they can afford insurance and savings, while staying on their same budget. And by helping them have a better life, you would earn an extra $2000 a month.

Well, what do you think?

◇◇◇◇◇

The more we hear these examples, the faster we will become comfortable giving our prospects the short answers to their questions.

But …

Did you notice this pattern?

Have you noticed how we answer question number three? We start by saying, "All you have to do is …"

Why?

Because these words signal to our prospects that we will give them the entire picture now. They don't have to wait for a sales presentation. We will sum up the activity with an easy explanation. This continues to relax our prospects so they don't revert to their salesman alarms.

Plus, what else happens? We say, "All you have to do is …" and our prospects think, "Hey, this is going to sound simple and doable. This will be something I can do or learn."

And finally, we end with these words. "And then you would earn an extra _____ a month." With these words, we remind our prospects that they want to earn this extra money every month!

Remember, we give our prospects a general idea of what they have to do. So don't worry about making this 100% accurate by adding an hour of details. All our prospects want at this time is a general idea of what they have to do to earn that money.

Time for some more examples.

Every one-minute presentation we create is only our current version. Over time, we tweak our one-minute presentations and improve their effectiveness. Maybe we get feedback from our prospects, input from our sponsors, or read a book that has an awesome way to describe our business. Don't be discouraged with our first attempts. They get better in time.

Our friend at work complains that the company underpays her. She wants to earn more, but doesn't see how at her position. We ask her, "So how much money would you like to earn?" She replies, "I want to earn $2000 a week in my career. Then I can do the things I want in life."

We then say, "Would you like to hear one way of earning that much money?" Of course she replies, "Yes!"

Here is the best part. We don't have to be nervous. We are only going to offer one more option to her choices. That means no rejection. All we have to do is give her the facts.

So we say, "I can give you a complete presentation, but it would take an entire minute. When can you set aside a whole minute?"

Done. She wants to hear the whole story now.

◇◇◇◇◇

Skincare.

If you want to earn an extra $2000 a week, you would have to do four things.

Number one: Don't change, continue to use your great communication skills to recommend and promote things you like. You are a master at that already.

Number two: We are in the anti-aging skincare business, and produce a skincare system that shows skin improvement in just 48 hours. Women hope that they can slow down or even reverse their skin's aging process. They want to see the difference in their skin.

Number three: All you have to do is get five women a week to try our inexpensive "Four-Day Skin Pack." Then, let them decide if they want to look younger forever, or continue aging as they are now. Over time, you will accumulate 150 or 200 happy customers who love what you did for their skin.

Number four: You have to sell your car. Because once you have over 60 customers, the company will give you a brand-new luxury car to drive. You will need room in your driveway for your new car.

And then you would earn an extra $2000 a week.

So, what do you think?

◇◇◇◇◇

Wait! There is another pattern.

Early in our one-minute presentation we say, "Don't change."

Why?

Because people hate change!

When we tell our prospects that they don't have to change, we can see their shoulders relax and the tension melt away from their faces. Everyone has some fear of change. Change could take us out of our comfort zone. Change has risks.

But if our prospects don't have to change, they think, "Oh yeah! Here is something I could do!"

Imagine what prospects would see in their minds if we told them they had to change! Oh my! They might see themselves going door-to-door begging for sales, or becoming over-caffeinated motivational speakers. But when our prospects hear that they don't have to change, these fears won't be created in their minds.

Now we are getting a different reaction from prospects than we did in the past. Instead of frowning faces and folded arms, our prospects feel excited about not having to change.

In the past, maybe we said something like this. Let's see if we can spot the flaw:

"In order to be successful in our business, the first thing you need to do is change. Yeah, you have to change your attitude, change your beliefs, change how you think, change your family, change your friends, change what you do on weekends, change what you do on weeknights. Yeah, you have to change."

Pretty easy to spot the flaw, right?

But when we start off with "Don't change," everything shifts in our prospects' minds.

Do you think that our aunt, our niece, our nephew, our co-worker would think, "If I don't have to change, wow! Excellent!" We've created a huge belief that they can do this business, because people have comfort zones.

When we leave our comfort zones, we are uncomfortable.

Let's see if we can spot the flaw in this presentation:

"Well, Mr. Prospect, in order for you to become successful, the first thing you need to do is get out of your comfort zone. Get a projector. Stand up, give a meeting in your aunt's home while she rolls on the floor, laughing hysterically. Get rejected over the phone. Meet strangers in the street. Just get out of your comfort zone."

When we start off with "Don't change," the prospect thinks, "Hey, here is an opportunity that I can take advantage of."

"Most people do network marketing every day, they just don't get paid for it."

If you have read our other books, you recognize this theme. It is human nature to want to recommend and promote good things that we find. All humans do this.

So if people recommend and promote things naturally every day, don't you think they deserve an opportunity to get paid for it? Why not let them have a choice?

They don't have to change. They do this already. This is an opportunity for them to collect.

"Don't change" is a very, very good thing to say.

How about a few more examples of one-minute presentations?

◇◇◇◇◇

Energy drinks.

If you want to earn an extra $200 a month without asking your boss for a raise, you would have to do these three things.

Number one: Don't change. Continue to recommend things that you like, such as your favorite snack or coffee shop.

Number two: We are in the energy drink business. People love energy drinks and buy them every day, but they would love to have a healthy option. Our "Lightning in a Can" energy drink is nutritious and good for them.

Number three: All you have to do is ask two people a day, "Would you like an energy drink that is also healthy?" At the end of one month, you will have enough people drinking our healthy energy drink that you will earn an extra $200 a month.

And the rest is up to you!

◇◇◇◇◇

Please notice that we do nothing special, nothing fantastic, nothing innovative, nothing super-intelligent. We mention the three or four things people have to do to earn the money we quoted them.

◇◇◇◇◇

Telecommunications.

If you want to earn an extra $200 a month, you would have to do these three things.

Number one: Don't change. Continue to recommend things that you like, such as your family dentist or a great place to go on vacation.

Number two: We are in the telecommunications business, which means we help people save a fortune on their cellphones and monthly charges.

Number three: All you have to do is help one new person join your team every month, and help them get their first five happy customers for our discounted cellphone package.

And then you would earn an extra $200 a month.

And that is it! The rest is up to you! So what do you think?

◇◇◇◇◇

(Okay, three closes in a row does sound a little high-pressure.)

◇◇◇◇◇

Discount travel.

If you want to earn an extra $400 a month, you would have to do these three things.

Number one: Don't change. Continue to recommend things that you like, such as your favorite things to do on weekends, or your favorite place to go on holiday.

Number two: We are in the discount travel business, which means we help families take five-star holidays for the price of a good hotel room. They have to take holidays anyway, so they might as well get better value for their money.

Number three: All you have to do is ask two people a day, "Would you like a great holiday this year without spending more?" At the end of two months, you will have enough regular family customers to earn an extra $400 a month.

And that is it! The rest is up to you!

◇◇◇◇◇

Looking clearer?

Simple is better. Clear is better. We have to avoid the temptation of trying to put all the good things we learned in the past into our presentation.

Here is an example of trying to **sell too much.**

◇◇◇◇◇

Health and wellness. (Oh, we are sounding vague already!)

If you want to create an extra full-time income, you need to do these three things.

Number one: Well, don't change a bit. Keep enjoying regular conversations with people, like you are doing with me. Make sure you are friendly and genuine, like you are now with me. Keep wanting to be healthy.

Number two: We are in the health and wellness business, which means that we have a patented, all-natural medical breakthrough, that is the result of 40 years of medical research by our award-winning scientists. This amazing discovery is changing people's lives.

Number three: All you would have to do is exactly what you are doing with me right now. Chat with people. Tell them about the science behind our products. Then show them our book of testimonials of other people who love our nutritional miracle and the effects it had on their mitochondria production. And, when they ask what you asked me, you would simply tell them what I am telling you now. Takes about a minute. And doing that, being friendly and genuine, wanting to be healthy, and chatting with a few people a day, five days a week, sharing with them what I shared you, and providing more details to those who want it ... you will create a full-time income in about two years.

Do you want to sign up?

◇◇◇◇◇

Ugh.

Can we see where this all went wrong? Let's see if we can improve this over-selling presentation and make it simpler. Here is an edited version. Think about which one would sound better to a prospect.

◇◇◇◇◇

Health and wellness.

If you want to earn a full-time income, you need to do these four things.

Number one: Don't change. Continue to talk about what you are passionate about.

Number two: We are in the health business, which means we help make sure that people can live longer. We all want to see our great-grandchildren get married. How do we do that? By taking one yellow super-pill a day that protects our body. Most people would love a chance to ensure that they could live longer.

Number three: All you would have to do is share this yellow pill solution with one person a day. Over the next two years, you will accumulate enough customers and people who want to share this yellow pill that you will create a full-time income.

Number four: Then you will have to decide if you want to keep your job, or share our yellow pill instead.

So what do you think?

◇◇◇◇◇

Better?

Sure. The difference is easy to see. All of our one-minute presentations are works in progress.

We should continue to fine-tune our presentations to make them simpler and clearer. Some words raise "salesman flags" and some words are too complicated. We become experts on our products and have an industry vocabulary, but our prospects might not know what we are talking about.

Don't despair if a one-minute presentation doesn't look or feel right when we start. Editing, testing, and improving will come over time.

For example, when we see our prospects' eyes glaze over, that would be a hint that we need to improve that section. Or, at a meeting, we hear another distributor describe things in a way that we love.

Just keep improving! Our one-minute presentation will get better and better over time. Soon we will love our one-minute presentation, and so will our prospects.

Would it be okay if we added a bit more rapport and some more magic words?

As we add other network marketing skills, our one-minute presentations become even more awesome. Let's start by adding some magic word skills to a presentation about an everyday necessity. Yes, a commodity.

◇◇◇◇◇

Utilities.

If you want to earn an extra $200 a month, you need to do these three things.

Number one: Don't change. Continue to recommend things that you like, such as your favorite restaurant or your favorite weekend hobby.

Number two: Well, you know how everyone gets an electricity bill, a gas bill, a telephone bill, a cellphone bill, and even an Internet bill? We show them how to get an instant discount on these bills by filling out a little online form that takes a few minutes.

Number three: All you would have to do is help one person a week get their discount by showing them how to fill out their online form. And then you would earn an extra $200 a month.

So would it be okay if you helped a few of your friends save money, and actually got paid for it too?

Antioxidants.

If you want to earn an extra $300 a month, you need to do these three things.

Number one: Don't change. Continue to recommend and promote things you like, such as your favorite doctor or place to go shopping.

Number two: Well, you know how we all hate growing old? We help people slow down the aging process so they stay younger ... longer. People like that. And they do this by taking these super-antioxidant capsules twice a day.

Number three: All you would have to do is find one person a week who wants to live longer and take care of his body by taking our super-antioxidant capsules. And, after two or three months, you would have enough people enjoying the super-antioxidant capsules to earn an extra $300 a month.

So would it be okay if you helped a few of your friends live longer, and actually got paid for it too?

◇◇◇◇◇

Are things getting clearer?

Guess what happens when I give a One-Minute Presentation Workshop? After someone demonstrates their new presentation, some people in the workshop say, "Hey! That sounds good. Talk to me during the break."

Why? Because there is a willing and eager market for our products and services. Many people can't wait to get what we have to offer. They wanted what we had to offer before, but we didn't explain it clearly. Now that we make our offer clear, they jump at the chance to buy or join.

All of these one-minute presentations are short. Can I make mine a little longer?

Of course. Just remember that shorter and simpler is better than longer and more complicated. We don't want our prospects to have to remember too many facts and details.

But let's do a few longer one-minute presentations to show how we can explain complicated compensation plans, in case this is what our prospects want.

◇◇◇◇◇

Cleansing diet.

If you want to earn an extra $5000 a month, you need to do these four things.

Number one: Don't change. Continue to recommend and promote things you like, such as your favorite donut shop or all-you-can-eat pizzeria.

Number two: Well, you know how hard it is to lose weight? We help overweight people manage their weight with a simple one-week cleanse that makes their bodies work more efficiently.

Number three: Sometime in your lifetime, you have to find four people who feel the same way about this business as you do. They want to earn a full-time income, or a good part-time income helping others manage their weight. Now, you don't have to find all four people right away. Pace yourself. One a month, one a decade, but sometime in your lifetime, find four people who feel the same way you do.

Number four: Between you, and everybody that you talk to, and everybody that they talk to, and everybody they talk to, forever and ever and ever, you eventually accumulate about 300 people that use the cleansing diet regularly. And then you will earn an extra $5000 a month.

And ... that is it!

Legal services.

If you want to earn an extra $500 a month, you need to do these four things.

Number one: Don't change. Continue to recommend and promote things you like, such as your favorite tax preparer or business supplier.

Number two: Well, you know how sometimes we have these little legal problems, but we don't fix them because lawyers are so expensive? We give families a lawyer on the telephone to sort out these little legal problems. These lawyers do it for a flat fee of $30 a month. Now people can't take advantage of us anymore.

Number three: Every Thursday night we have an online presentation about how these legal services work. The presentation takes 18 minutes. And all you have to do is make sure you have two or three people watch this presentation every week.

Number four: Usually, about half the people who watch the presentation say, "Yes, this is exactly what I need." You will then help them go online and fill out the membership form. Plus, you can answer any questions they might still have.

And then you would earn an extra $500 a month.

And ... that is it!

Air purifiers.

If you want to earn an extra $500 a month, you need to do these three things.

Number one: Don't change. Continue to recommend and promote things you like, such as your favorite sports team, favorite car brand, or favorite brand of beer.

Number two: We are in the air purification business, which means we show people how to have fresh, clean air inside their homes, even though our city has record-high air pollution levels. Now they can breathe better and get a good night's sleep too.

Number three: All you have to do is demonstrate our air purification filter to five or six people every month, so they can see and experience the difference. Then, let them decide. About half of the people want an air purifier immediately. And then you would earn an extra $500 a month.

And the rest is up to you!

◇◇◇◇◇

See another pattern?

Notice how we wrap up our presentation with the words:

"And then you would earn an extra _____ a month."

This is a great way to signal to our prospects that we are finishing our presentation. Even though we tell them that we will finish in one minute, most won't believe us. So when we finish in less than one minute, they are shocked ... and impressed!

Plus, this phrase summarizes the big benefit that our prospects want. We remind them of the money they can earn. That was the point of our presentation to them, wasn't it?

Feel a little bit nervous doing this the first time?

That means we are human. Of course we will be a bit nervous when we first try this.

But what happens the second time we give a one-minute presentation? Maybe still a bit nervous.

The third time we try? We feel better.

The fourth time we try? Relieved. This was so easy.

The fifth time we try? We are excited because we see how much our prospects appreciate that the presentation was short and to the point.

The sixth time we try? It feels so natural. Soon we'll be able to do this in our sleep.

While we improve our one-minute presentation, remember these facts:

1. If our one-minute presentation is awful, it is all over in less than a minute.

2. The worst one-minute presentation is usually better than a perfect 30-minute presentation.

3. If we do a terrible one-minute presentation, our prospect will think, "Wow. You are terrible. I can do better than that. I will make a fortune!"

A WORD ABOUT
THREE-WAY CALLS.

Telephone advice from me? Well, I don't like using the telephone. Decades ago, when I first started, the company leaders had a little joke about me. They said, "Never get Big Al on a three-way telephone call with a prospect. Not only will the prospect not join, but the distributor will quit."

I don't think I'm that bad. However, I still limit my time on the telephone. If we call a referral, we could keep it short with the one-minute presentation. Here is an example.

Distributor: "Hello, is this Mr. Referral?"

Mr. Referral: "Yeah."

Distributor: "Your name was given to me by a friend of yours. And wow! Have I got a wonderful opportunity for you."

Mr. Referral: "Can't you hear me chewing my food? I am having dinner."

Distributor: "Oh, sorry. I can give you a complete presentation, but it would take an entire minute. When could you set aside a whole minute?"

Mr. Referral: "It's going to take me a minute to finish chewing and swallowing. Do it now so you never have to call me back."

Pretty amazing, isn't it? Even if we are terrible on the telephone, the one-minute presentation can help.

But back to those three-way calls.

Why do we make three-way calls with our team?

Three-way calls with prospects can help us with credibility. When we are new, it sounds better when a third party gives the presentation to our prospect.

But we can grow from there.

The biggest reason for three-way calls with new distributors is that they can't explain their business properly. They don't know where to start, where to end ... or even when to stop talking. In the next example, we can see how the one-minute presentation can help.

Imagine that you are like me, uncomfortable with long telephone conversations. One day your distributor calls you and says, "Hey, I have a hot prospect on the line with me now. Please tell him all about our opportunity."

Yikes! No background, no preparation. So you get on the call, do the best you can and say, "I can give you a complete presentation, but it would take an entire minute. When could you set aside a whole minute?"

The prospect says, "Right now. Tell me over the telephone."

You give your simple one-minute presentation and finish by saying, "And the rest is up to you. So let me get off the telephone now so the two of you can visit. Thanks for your time."

Done.

What is the prospect thinking? "That wasn't so hard. I could learn to say that."

What is the distributor thinking? "I don't need to call my sponsor anymore. I could learn to say that."

The one-minute presentation is a great way to help new distributors become competent quickly.

What would be a slightly better introduction on a three-way call?

We don't say anything at the beginning of the call. The distributor starts his call with his prospect by saying:

"Hi, John. I told you at work I would get my sponsor on the telephone with you for one minute, so he could tell you what he told me. And, you might want to start a business just like we did. But anyway, here is my sponsor."

It is not hard to get anyone to listen to us if we promise that our side of the conversation will only be a minute. That makes three-way call appointments easy.

How long will it take to train a new distributor to use their one-minute presentation?

Once our new distributor discovers the one-minute presentation, it is time to get some experience. This is one way to get that experience fast.

We can call our new distributor and say, "Well, we are going to start now. Make a list of five people that we can call tomorrow night. At 6:30 PM, I will get on the telephone with you and help make the calls."

The next evening, we get on the telephone with our new distributor. We call the first prospect, then the next prospect, etc. We give the one-minute presentation while our new distributor listens.

By 7:00 PM, we're finished. Done.

We can go back to watching television. Our new distributor can go back to his or her spouse and say, "Guess what? I am done for the evening. Out of the five calls, three were home and answered their telephones. One person wants to join."

This is one way we can build our business efficiently without spending hours on the phone.

Is it always this easy?

"Is it always this easy? We give one-minute presentations and prospects throw money at us?"

At the end of our one-minute presentation, our prospects have these three choices:

Choice #1: I want to join your business.

Choice #2: I don't want to join your business.

Choice #3: Your business sounds good, but I have a question or two.

Not too complicated.

So how do we handle these choices in real life?

Choice #1 is easy. They want to join. We enroll them. Done.

Choice #2 is easy. They don't want to join. We continue our conversation about other topics.

Choice #3 requires that we continue our conversation. Our prospects have questions, and we need to answer these questions.

Answering questions.

Here is our philosophy about questions.

1. When prospects ask questions, that means they want to join. Think about it. If our prospects didn't want to join, why would they ask for more information? They want more facts to support their desire to join.

2. It is polite to answer our prospects' questions as clearly as we can.

3. If our answer disqualifies them, that is okay. It is not for them at this time. That's fair.

This will be nice and easy.

Our job is to answer our prospects' questions as honestly and as straight-forward as we can. We don't have to learn special rejection, manipulation analysis, or advanced neural linguistic programming techniques. We answer their questions. Our prospects are adults. They can decide what is best for their lives.

What kind of questions will our prospects ask?

Let's look at some common questions. Please note that the answers to these questions are simple. Can we learn additional ways to answer in the future? Of course. As long as they are honest and direct, they will be fine.

Question:
"Well, what is the name of your company?"

We answer with the name of our company. Done. Our prospect can then ask another question. Or, maybe our answer disqualified our prospect. Our negative prospect says, "Oh, I can't join any companies that start with a vowel. Vowels are evil."

Done.

No need for us to go further. Time to discuss another subject. Now that is a relief. We don't have to fight the objection by saying, "Well, some of our products start with consonants. Not everything starts with a vowel. I heard that there might be a new alphabet coming soon."

Our prospects have choices. We can't be responsible for their choices and what those choices will mean in their lives.

Question:
"So how much does it cost to get started?"

We tell them. Our answer could be something like this.

"$99 to join. That gets you started, registered, and more. Then, you can buy as little or as much product as you want."

Or, we could say, "It is not like opening a store at the local mall. It won't cost you $50,000 and a second mortgage on your home. It costs $999 to join, and that includes your training and our secret decoder ring."

No need to hide the cost. Anyone serious enough to start a business knows it will cost some money. Plus, tell them now. How long do you think we would keep it a secret anyway? They are not going to be in our business three or four years from now, and suddenly say, "Oh, so that is how much it costs to get started."

What if our prospect reacts to our answer by saying, "No way! Are you crazy? Why should I pay that much to get started? I can buy a fast-food franchise for $49."

This person is not the business genius we want leading our team. We can now choose to talk about another subject.

But you might be wondering, "Why don't we tell our prospects how much it costs during our one-minute presentation?"

Good question. Well, we could include this in our presentation. There are many things we can include in our presentation, but consider this. If our prospect doesn't want to join, why bother him with all the useless data about the cost to join? There is no need to waste time explaining startup costs when our prospect does not want to join.

And if our prospect wants to join at the end of our one-minute presentation, he can ask how much it costs to join.

Question:
"Well, how much money have you made so far?"

There are enticement rules in many countries, so if we made a fortune, we wouldn't even be allowed to tell our prospects. But let's imagine we made … zero. We haven't earned our first dollar. What could we say?

"I haven't earned anything yet. It is a business, not a job. I am hoping to start making some good money in about six months. Then, I will use that money to take a cruise. I was wondering if you wanted to join and build a business with me, or not. We could take that cruise together. If you are not interested in this business, no problem. Could I get your mailing address? Because I would like to send you a postcard from the cruise."

Questions are easy.

Answer the best we can. Later, we can get better. For now, relax. Being honest and direct is the best way to go.

We could do many more question examples, but the answers are always the same. Honest and direct.

Only interested people ask questions, so let's welcome questions.

If our prospects are not interested, we give them a chance to tell us "no" when we finish our one-minute presentation. Remember those easy closes?

1. So, what do you think?

2. And that is it.

3. The rest is up to you.

Prospects can tell us "no" at this point, and we don't have to worry about any questions.

But what about objections?

Prospects create objections based upon what we say and do. If we change what we say and do, we will get fewer objections, or no objections.

Skeptical? Consider this example.

A prospect walks down the street. Suddenly the prospect throws his hands up in the air and shouts, "It's a pyramid!"

Well, that doesn't happen in real life. In real life, the pyramid objection comes from something that we say or something that we do.

So let's rethink objections. Most of the objections we have gotten in the past will go away when we do something different. Many objections are simply ways of getting out of the conversation gracefully for our prospects.

However, with the one-minute presentation, we give our prospects many opportunities to leave the conversation. There is no need for our prospects to come up with ridiculous objections so they can escape.

Now we can relax. We won't have to learn answers to most of the objections we heard in the past.

And on the positive side, there will be fewer objections because we are only having a conversation with our prospects. We are not giving the full 30-minute sales presentations that make them want to escape.

Remember, most of our initial objections will go away. Why? Because we told our prospects that our presentation would last an entire minute. Our prospects think, "I don't want to give you an objection, because it might take you longer than one minute to answer that objection. Go ahead with your one-minute presentation now."

Expanding our one-minute presentation.

When we're talking about larger incomes, we need a different way of explaining what prospects will need to do. We can be a bit creative.

Remember, the one-minute presentation is designed to give prospects a general overview. We help them make a preliminary decision:

1. "Yes, I'd like to join."

2. "No, I don't want to join."

3. "I have a few questions."

We don't have to include all the details and disclaimers for each data point presented. At this point, the prospects want to know if they should continue the conversation or not.

Let's give our prospects what they want. Later, our prospects might ask us for all the information we've been wanting to tell them. But not now.

How can we explain bigger incomes?

We will start with an example, and then make it better.

◇◇◇◇◇

If you want to earn an extra $5000 a month, you need to do these three things.

Number one: Don't change. Continue to recommend and promote things you like, such as your favorite beverage, or weekend activities.

Number two: We are in the pet business. We make pet owners happy by helping their pets live longer. We do this by providing special pet nutrition supplements and food for their pets.

Number three: All you have to do is get four or five leaders to build a small team of distributors who love pets. Teach these leaders to teach their distributors how to talk to pet owners. And, if they do their job right, in less than a year, you could be earning $5000 extra every month.

So, what do you think?

◇◇◇◇◇

Well, technically this explains our business. But when we do step number three - explaining what they have to do to earn that money - it gets pretty clumsy. So how can we fix that?

Let's go back to the purpose of a one-minute presentation. We want to give our prospects an understanding of what we do. We don't have to explain everything in microscopic detail. So is there a better way to explain step number three in the above example?

Think about this from our prospects' perspective. We asked them to get four or five leaders. They have no idea what a leader is! What we say is accurate, but our prospects will not understand. Is there another way to explain leaders that they could grasp?

Next, we asked them to build a small team of distributors. At this point, they may not even know what a distributor is or what a distributor does. Again, we are being unclear.

To solve this, we will describe a leader as someone who "feels" the same way that they do. Somebody who loves pets and wants to help pet owners be happy when their pets live a longer, healthier life. This is what they need to know at this point in their decision-making process.

Here is how step number three will sound now.

"All you have to do, between you, and everybody you talk to, and everybody they talk to, and everybody they talk to, forever and ever and ever, is find four or five people who feel the same way that you do. People who love pets, and would like to earn a full-time income helping pets live longer, happier lives."

What have we done?

We told our prospects that they only have to find four or five people who "feel" like they do. And they don't have to find all four or five people immediately. They can pace themselves.

Now, if they find four or five people who feel like they do, these people would be leaders, or potential leaders. These people are excited about sharing the mission of helping pets live longer.

If they had four or five leaders on their team, they should be earning at least $5000 a month. This is an easier explanation for our prospects to understand. So let's see how this would sound in our one-minute presentation.

◇◇◇◇◇

If you want to earn an extra $5000 a month, you need to do these three things.

Number one: Don't change. Continue to recommend and promote things you like, such as your favorite beverage, or weekend activities.

Number two: We are in the pet business. We make pet owners happy by helping their pets live longer. We do this by providing special pet nutrition supplements and food for their pets.

Number three: All you have to do, between you, and everybody you talk to, and everybody they talk to, and everybody they talk to, forever and ever and ever, is find four or five people who feel the same way that you do. People who love pets, and would like to earn a full-time income helping pets live happier lives.

And then you would earn an extra $5000 a month.

So, what do you think?

◇◇◇◇◇

Our goal is to communicate our business clearly. Sometimes too much information confuses prospects. This creates an unclear, and unfair business explanation.

Let's do another example.

◇◇◇◇◇

If you want to earn an extra $5000 a month, you need to do these three things.

Number one: Don't change. Continue to recommend and promote things you like, such as your favorite music or car brand.

Number two: We are in the vitamin business. Most people want vitamins, but they don't know which ones to take, and they don't want to waste their money. We show them what will work for them so they don't waste their money.

Number three: All you have to do is, sometime in your lifetime, locate four or five people who also have a passion for nutrition. Teach them how they can have a part-time business helping their friends have better nutrition. Now, you don't have to find all four or five people right away. Pace yourself. One a week, one a month, or one a year. And then you would earn an extra $5000 a month.

So what do you think?

◇◇◇◇◇

Find four or five people who have a passion for nutrition. That sounds doable. And, there is no time limit. This gives our prospects an idea of what they have to do to earn $5000 a month.

What else can I do?

Describing bigger incomes is one way we can adjust our one-minute presentations.

If our company had a car bonus, we could add that.

If our company had free holidays that we could win, we could add that.

We could include these benefits in step number three, or we could add an additional step to include that benefit. Here are a few examples.

◇◇◇◇◇

Number three: All you have to do is, sometime in your lifetime, locate four or five people who have a passion for helping others put their finances in order. Teach these people how using insurance and mutual funds can help the average family succeed.

Number four: Line up some babysitters. Because not only will you be earning an extra $5000 a month, but the company will also send you on an all-expense-paid one-week holiday at least once a year.

And the rest is up to you.

◇◇◇◇◇

So let's do one that offers a car bonus.

◇◇◇◇◇

Number three: All you have to do is, sometime in your lifetime, locate four or five people who want a good part-time income, or even a full-time income. Show them how they can earn that extra money helping their friends and neighbors save money on their utilities. This will earn you an extra $5000 a month.

Number four: Sell your car. You will have to make room in your driveway for the new car the company awards their serious workers.

And the rest is up to you.

How about one more for diet products? We will make this one fun.

Number three: All you have to do is, sometime in your lifetime, locate five overweight people who want to lose weight, keep it off forever, and tell everyone about their success. Finding overweight people is easy. They are hard to miss. But we will have to check if they are serious about losing weight.

Number four: You will have to get a new passport and driver's license because you will look different. And, you will invest an extra day or two every month looking for new, fashionable clothes to fit your new body. But with that extra $5000 a month, shopping will be a lot more fun.

The rest is up to you!

Make it easy. We don't want to tell prospects:

"And all you have to is find 20 qualified customers, each using three of the services down two legs through three generations. Each primary leg should have two other people that duplicate the same thing by signing up on a form A14."

Well, we may not be that bad, but sometimes our explanations sound cryptic to prospects.

And then, if our prospects are interested, we can leisurely go through all the tiny details of our business.

WHY DISTRIBUTORS DON'T GIVE PRESENTATIONS.

Here are four reasons why distributors don't present their program to their warm market of friends and relatives:

1. They don't understand how their program works. We made our initial explanation far too complicated.

2. They don't know how to present their business. They didn't attend training. They have never been salespeople.

3. They fear rejection. They think a presentation is a win-lose proposal. We didn't tell them that our mission is to give prospects another choice in their lives.

4. They don't believe in their business. They think a person has to be a high-pressure salesman, and they know their warm market wouldn't want that.

Want to solve these four problems?

Try making our presentations simple. We recommend a one-minute presentation for new distributors.

- A simple presentation is clear and easy for the prospect and the distributor to understand.

- A simple presentation is easy to learn and doesn't require a three-hour training session.

- A simple presentation helps reduce rejection. The prospect doesn't build up sales resistance if the presentation takes only one minute.

- And finally, it is easy to believe in our program if we find it easy for anyone to explain.

The one-minute presentation solves these four problems. By reducing our presentations to only the most pertinent points, everyone is happy. If our prospects are interested, they can get additional details now, or at their first training session. But getting additional details is our prospects' choice, not ours.

Most prospects are happy with the short, clear, to-the-point one-minute presentation.

We can use the one-minute presentation anywhere!

This short presentation solves the problem of how we talk to someone when we are not sitting down at an official, face-to-face presentation. We don't need a flipchart, we don't need PowerPoint slides, and we don't even need a pen or paper. This frees us up to give a presentation anywhere at any time.

Let's look at some places where our one-minute presentation would be an appropriate option.

1. When we pick up our children from school, we don't have time to sit down with the other parents and do a presentation with our catalog.

2. We are waiting to be seated at a restaurant. The maître d' comments, "Not many people come here at 4:00 PM. So what kind of business are you in?"

3. We are on a three-way call with our prospect. The prospect says, "I am busy with the family. What is this all about?"

4. While standing in line at the bank, the couple in front of us starts a conversation with us. They ask us, "So what kind of business are you in?"

5. On our flight back home, the person sitting next to us says this: "You seem so happy. Tell me, what kind of work do you do?"

6. We invite our cousin to the local opportunity meeting. Our cousin hesitates and says, "First, tell me what this is all about. I don't want to waste a whole evening hearing about something that I am not interested in."

7. At the coffee machine at work, your best friend comments, "Yeah, I would like to be in business with you. But first, tell me a little about this new business you started."

8. When we don't want to call prospects back. We know what to expect when we call prospects back. They say, "Oh, I haven't had a chance to review the literature and video yet." The one-minute presentation gets decisions … now.

Let's use our imagination. Whenever we feel a bit shy, or don't want to look like a pushy salesman, the one-minute presentation is a great solution. No longer will we panic and think, "Where do I start? Do I give them a business card and run? Do I show them the new company video? Do I loan them some literature? Do I talk about my products? Do I call my sponsor?"

We can tell the whole story in less than one minute. No rejection. Just the facts. No more pressure on us. Total relief!

Should I use the one-minute presentation all of the time?

No. The one-minute presentation is only one way of presenting our opportunity. It is not the only way.

Maybe we're thinking, "Wait a minute. If we can do the whole presentation in one minute, why are opportunity meetings so long?" Good question.

Here is why opportunity meetings are longer. Imagine that tonight's opportunity meeting starts at 8:00 PM. Our guest drives one hour to attend. Our guest also knows that it will take him another hour to drive home. We start our meeting. It is only one minute long. How would our guest feel? Pretty bad. And how would our guest feel if he arrived one minute late? Really bad.

Prospects expect opportunity meetings to be longer. We will have to add some filler to stretch our meeting out. :)

We can fill up those minutes with testimonials, slides, and compensation plan explanations.

What about engineers and accountants?

They may want more information and all of the details. But, don't give them these details first. Give the one-minute presentation first.

Now they have a choice.

1. Not interested.

2. More details.

If they are not interested, we are done. We save both their time and our time.

If they want more details, then we can set up camp. We can answer questions and explain details into the late hours of the evening.

Use our judgment.

Bottom line? We want to serve our prospects as best we can. The one-minute presentation is one way to do a presentation, but not the only way.

However, we might find the one-minute presentation is our preferred method of explaining our business.

Here are a few of the benefits of the one-minute presentation.

1. We don't have to give prospects literature to take home and study.

2. Our prospects don't have to go to websites that have 100 different information links.

3. No one has to sit through a one-hour opportunity presentation unless they want to.

4. If prospects make a "yes" decision from our one-minute presentation, then opportunity meetings become their first training sessions.

5. We can tell people directly over the telephone what our business does. We don't have to keep secrets.

6. We can answer our prospects' three basic questions quickly:

   Question #1: "What kind of business are you in?"

   Question #2: "How much money can I make?"

   Question #3: "Exactly what do I have to do to earn this money?"

7. No one has to watch boring opportunity videos.

8. When a prospect calls, we don't have to be evasive. We can answer honestly and directly. Our prospect will be happy.

9. The one-minute presentation can also be the perfect way to end a business opportunity meeting or a home presentation. Prospects like a clear summary.

10. We can prevent no-shows. Prospects fail to keep appointments or attend opportunity meetings as promised. When we give the one-minute presentation, we remove our prospects' fear of the unknown. Now they are more likely to keep their commitment.

11. We don't need to wait 45 minutes to get a decision. We can get a "yes" or "no" answer in one minute.

12. No more long telephone calls with endless conversation. We can get to the point with prospects quickly and efficiently.

FINALLY ...

"I can give you a complete presentation, but it would take an entire minute. When could you set aside a whole minute?"

Let's put these two sentences to use now.

Why?

Because if we don't use these two magic sentences, we will be sentenced to a lifetime of tension and rejection, trying to get prospects to listen to our presentations.

And if we don't answer our prospects' three basic questions, our prospects won't understand how network marketing can change their lives.

Good luck sponsoring!

THANK YOU.

Thank you for purchasing and reading this book. I hope you found some ideas that will work for you.

Before you go, would it be okay if I asked a small favor? Would you take just one minute and leave a short review of this book online? Your review can help others choose what they will read next. It would be greatly appreciated by many fellow readers.

I travel the world 240+ days each year.
Let me know if you want me to stop in your
area and conduct a live Big Al training.

→ **BigAlSeminars.com** ←

FREE Big Al Training Audios
Magic Words for Prospecting

plus Free eBook and the Big Al Report!

→ **BigAlBooks.com/free** ←

MORE BIG AL BOOKS

The Four Color Personalities for MLM
The Secret Language for Network Marketing

Learn the skill to quickly recognize the four personalities and how to use magic words to translate your message.

Ice Breakers!
How To Get Any Prospect To Beg You For A Presentation

Create unlimited Ice Breakers on-demand. Your distributors will no longer be afraid of prospecting, instead, they will love prospecting.

How To Get Instant Trust, Belief, Influence and Rapport!
13 Ways To Create Open Minds By Talking To The Subconscious Mind

Learn how the pros get instant rapport and cooperation with even the coldest prospects. The #1 skill every new distributor needs.

First Sentences for Network Marketing
How To Quickly Get Prospects On Your Side

Attract more prospects and give more presentations with great first sentences that work.

How to Follow Up With Your Network Marketing Prospects
Turn Not Now Into Right Now!

Use the techniques in this book to move your prospects forward from "Not Now" to "Right Now!"

How To Prospect, Sell And Build Your Network Marketing Business With Stories

If you want to communicate effectively, add your stories to deliver your message.

26 Instant Marketing Ideas To Build Your Network Marketing Business

176 pages of amazing marketing lessons and case studies to get more prospects for your business immediately.

How To Build Network Marketing Leaders

Volume One: Step-By-Step Creation Of MLM Professionals

This book will give you the step-by-step activities to actually create leaders.

How To Build Network Marketing Leaders

Volume Two: Activities And Lessons For MLM Leaders

You will find many ways to change people's viewpoints, to change their beliefs, and to reprogram their actions.

Complete list at BigAlBooks.com

ABOUT THE AUTHORS

Keith Schreiter has 20+ years of experience in network marketing and MLM. He shows network marketers how to use simple systems to build a stable and growing business.

So, do you need more prospects? Do you need your prospects to commit instead of stalling? Want to know how to engage and keep your group active? If these are the types of skills you would like to master, you will enjoy his "how-to" style.

Keith speaks and trains in the U.S., Canada, and Europe.

Tom "Big Al" Schreiter has 40+ years of experience in network marketing and MLM. As the author of the original "Big Al" training books in the late '70s, he has continued to speak in over 80 countries on using the exact words and phrases to get prospects to open up their minds and say "YES."

His passion is marketing ideas, marketing campaigns, and how to speak to the subconscious mind in simplified, practical ways. He is always looking for case studies of incredible marketing campaigns that give usable lessons.

As the author of numerous audio trainings, Tom is a favorite speaker at company conventions and regional events.

51721404R00078

Made in the USA
San Bernardino, CA
30 July 2017